Library and Archives Canada Cataloguing in Publication

Livingston, Kamarie, 1968-, photographer
Healing : practical ways to find your own way / photos by Kamarie Livingston ; text by Harry van Bommel.
Photo book with short texts.
ISBN 978-1-55307-090-0 (paperback)
1. Nature, Healing power of. 2. Mental healing. 3. Nature--Pictorial works. I. Van Bommel, Harry, author II. Title.

R723.L59 2016 615.8'528 C2015-908311-7

To contact the photographer, write:
Kamarie Livingston
10225 Wildwood Road
Bloomington, MN 55437 USA
kamarie.livingston@gmail.com

To contact the author, write or call:
Harry van Bommel
Legacies Inc.
11 Miniot Circle, Scarborough, Ontario
CANADA M1K 2K1
(416) 264-4665 harry@legacies.ca

Healing

Practical Ways to Find Your Own Way

Photos by
Kamarie Livingston

Text by
Harry van Bommel

A Canada 150 Book
Legacies Inc.
Toronto 2016

Kamarie dedicates this book to her husband and love of her life, Michael, whose w
presence is a form of healing for her every single day. This project would not have happened without his love and support.

She also dedicates this book to her mother and best friend, Sonja Davie, without whom she would not have been able to make it this far in this journey at all.

Harry dedicates this book to Janet, Joanna, Bram, family and friends who each possess a thoughtful, healing presence.

Courage is not the absence of fear –
it's inspiring others to move beyond it.
Nelson Mandela

6 Introduction
10 Ten Commandments of Healing
15 Healing Nature
16 Healing Relationships
17 Healing Presence
18 Healing Breaths
20 Healing Attitudes
21 Healing Places & Spaces
22 Healing Movements
23 Healing Inspiration
24 Healing – Kamarie's Thoughts
29 Healing Spirit
30 Healing Thoughts
31 Healing Touch
32 Healing Care
33 Healing Prayers & Meditations
34 Healing Perspectives
34 Healing Smiles
35 Healing Destiny
36 Healing – The Universal Rule
38 Healing Music
38 Healing Listening
39 Healing Courage
40 Healing Stories
41 Healing Memories
42 Healing Reading & Writing
43 Healing Stories
44 Healing – What Next?
45 About the Author & Photographer

Introduction

There are so many definitions of "healing." For our purposes, it means 'to make whole again.' To feel complete as you are regardless of circumstances. To feel that you have and are enough. Enough love. Enough support. Enough gratitude. Enough of yourself to give to others.

Let us begin with a story. Mr. G was a 70 year-old man who had a large, disfiguring tumor of the nasal cavity. The tumor covered most of his face from his eyes to his chin. He was in his last months of life in a palliative care unit at a hospital in London, Ontario. He was getting excellent care and was surrounded by a loving family and his supportive faith community. His pain and symptoms were well managed. He was able to enjoy the company of family and friends. But he wanted to die.

Although the tumor had eaten away his nose and mouth and, therefore, he could not speak, he made it clear that he wanted to die. He wrote: "Every time someone walks into my room, they look at my tumor and they cringe. They suffer on my behalf. They are frightened, pitying or disgusted. I can't do it to them anymore. I can't watch them look at me. Please help me to die."

His wife of many years who loved him dearly agreed that she wished he could die to avoid this daily suffering.

This man had a six-year older granddaughter. She really wanted to visit him at the hospital but her parents, grandparents and the palliative care team wanted to save her from seeing him as he was now. They wanted her to remember him as he had been — as if he had already died.

Six-year old girls can be quite persistent. She would not give up until her mother, Mr. G's daughter, agreed to let her visit. First the child had to undergo a conversation with several members of the palliative care team, who were still not sure she should visit, to prepare her for what she was going to see.

Once she tolerated as much as she could from the team, they allowed her to visit her grandfather. They pointed out his room and she rushed down the hall, pushed open the door with that great energy of six-year olds, ran up to her grandfather and gave him a big hug and said, "I love you Grandpa. Please don't go."

It took a six-year girl to teach her grandparents, her parents, and the palliative care team what it means to see someone as 'whole.' To see them as complete, as is, right in this moment. To recognize the humanity and the person you love beneath the superficial tumor or other things that discomfort so many adults. She saw her grandfather while everyone else saw a patient dying with cancer.

So this book is about seeing yourself and those you love as whole; complete as is. To see yourself as 'healed' after you have thoughtfully put yourself back together; as the whole you for this moment.

The book looks at thoughts and actions that can bring you to that place where wholeness is possible more often than not. Your life won't be perfect, of course, nor will healing necessarily lead to a complete cure or recovery. But by healing yourself and allowing others to help, you can feel whole in ways that you might never have experienced before. Healing, even when you are sick, is possible because you have control over how you see yourself and how you help others to see you.

We hope this book provides some ideas to help you heal. It combines the visual with ideas and meditations and prayers that can be learned regardless of one's faith and beliefs. The book can be used in several ways:

1. Just enjoy the photos. They are most helpful when you look at them slowly and carefully. Look at specific details of color, textures, its perspective, where the light is shining from and even the sounds, smells and tastes that were probably there at the time the photo was taken. Use your imagination to visualize what is just to the left and just to the right of the photo, out of view of the scene. What might be behind the photographer as she took the shot?

2. Read the words and follow the instructions, if there are any. You can certainly match different photos to whichever words appeal to you most or create a visual image in your mind.

3. Memorize the photos and/or words to use when the book is not available. For example, one of the most frightening experiences for people is being in the hospital. If you cannot wear your glasses, or look at the book, you can use your memory to provide the visual image and words to provide you comfort.

Another example, is when you are completely alone. Many former prisoners of war repeated poems, spiritual texts and other phrases over and over again to provide a sense of 'home, ' family, safety and healing in a horrible situation.

These are also the times when we feel that we cannot control our mind's thoughts. We feel powerless by our own run-away thoughts. We may even feel like we are 'loosing our mind' to an outside force.

These are the times when we need to take control of our thoughts and feelings. These are the times when using some techniques in this book will let you concentrate on what your mind brings forward in ways that takes away the anxious elements of those fears.

These are the times when repetitive words and images can help us regain control of our thoughts. May some of what we present here be helpful to you during the days to come.

TEN COMMANDMENTS OF HEALING

Dr. Balfour Mount is a patient, family caregiver and a pioneer physician in hospice palliative care internationally who coined the phrase 'palliative care.' His humility allows him to learn from others and his generosity to share that learning with us.

How important to attend to the insights of our teachers, that is to say, the men, women and children who have been our patients and their families. We are indebted to them for the legacy they leave us. Paradoxically, their end-of-life lessons have not been about dying, but about living.

What is the core lesson they have taught us? It is that healing is the central goal of life. I am not speaking of *physical* healing, a person can die healed: what I mean by 'healing' is a shift in our quality of life away from anguish and suffering, toward an experience of integrity, wholeness and inner peace. Jon Kabat-Zinn defines healing as a process of adaptation, a "coming to terms with things as they are."

The psyche, it would seem, has an intrinsic tendency toward healing, a will-to-wholeness, as it were. How can we experience that? How can you and I find inner peace in the turmoil of each day? Let me summarize our patients' message to us as "*The 10 Commandments of Healing*." They are:

1) BE TRULY PRESENT TO THIS MOMENT. Healing, like love, celebration, awe, wonder and ecstasy, happens in the now, in the present moment, free from ruminations of the past and fears about the future. As Oliver Wendell Holmes stated it, "What lies behind us and what lies before us are tiny matters compared to what lies within us."

   And yet I find that I spend most of my time preoccupied with the past or the future. I must come into the present; be aware of the persons and things that are around me right now.

2) TRUST. Healing involves letting go, a leap of faith, 'diving not drowning' as Carl Jung expressed it. Lou Gherig's disease patient Phil Simmons called it 'learning to fall.' We fall **from** head, **to** heart; **from** egoism and our carefully constructed defense mechanisms, we fall **into** forgiveness of ourselves and others, the realization of the staggering potential of our essential selves, and an awareness of healing connections.

We may experience these connections at four levels: a sense of connection to self (Carl Jung's individuation); connection to others (Martin Buber's 'I-thou' relating); connection to the world perceived through our senses (as with music, or the grandeur of nature); and connection to ultimate meaning, however perceived by that person: God, the Other, the Cosmos, the More, the unity of all things.

3) ATTEND TO YOUR WHOLE-PERSON NEEDS. According to the time-honored metaphoric classification, we are 'body, mind, and spirit', or, 'body, spirit and soul', depending on you preference. We must care for our needs in **each** of these domains **every** day.

4) OPEN TO DEEPER RELATING. Recall that our inner life is relational in its expression. It is reflected in how we relate at domains levels noted above.

Within your religious or wisdom tradition seek out teachers who speak from personal experience, not dogma. Go to depth. As C.S. Lewis observed, "The process of living seems to consist in coming to realize truths so ancient and simple that, if stated, they sound like barren platitudes." Lewis continues, "They cannot sound otherwise to those who have not had the relevant experience: that is why there is no real teaching of such truths possible and every generation starts from scratch."

5) LISTEN TO YOUR INTUITION. As Joseph Campbell put it, "Follow your bliss."

6) **CREATE.** Identify things you like to do. Make time for your creative side each day.

7) **DEVELOP SELF-REFLECTIVE SKILLS.** Monitor self, noting your thoughts and feelings. They are **not** reality. They are your **response to** reality. Let go of them and come back to your center of calm. Work on becoming self-aware with questioning that asks, "What is my personality type and how does that influence how I feel about myself, how I relate to others and to the situations I find myself in? What are my defenses - the walls I build to protect myself, but that also imprison me?"

8) **BE GENTLE WITH YOURSELF.** Progression toward healing is slow. Indeed, the goal is never reached. The journey is everything. You are a unique experiment in creation, with a particular potential to contribute to this world. What is it that you alone can do, **must** do, if you are to fully express your potential?

9) **THINK SMALL.** Give up illusions of control. Recognize that we are all in the same boat, **exactly** the same boat. The ego-driven values of Western culture ('I am number one'; the need for wealth, power and control; the distrust of all but the physical; the need to be the best in the world in what you do) stand in the way of healing.

Avoid power; neutralize the fantasies it creates in situations where it is bestowed on you. Humility and openness are essential antecedents to healing; joy, peace and a sense of connectedness its products.

10) **CELEBRATE.** In the direst of circumstances, boundless peace is to be found within. Recall Viktor Frankl's hard-won observation, "Everything can be taken from a man but one thing: the last of human freedoms – to choose one's attitude in any given set of circumstances, to choose one's own way." If Frankl can find life worth celebrating in Auschwitz, chances are I can find my cup half full, perhaps full to overflowing, here and now.

These are the 10 commandments of healing that our teachers have given us.

Healing involves a process of opening, slowing, centering, trusting, hoping and accepting. It involves recognizing the potential that still remains, in spite of all that has been lost.

For each of us the path toward healing will be different. The most certain path I have found is meditation. I do not imply that it is the only path. It is just the only path I know. The purpose of meditation, in its many forms, is to create alert awareness with a still mind and presence to the moment.

There is no shortcut to healing. Carl Jung put it this way, "The attainment of wholeness requires one to stake one's whole being. Nothing less will do; there can be no easier conditions, no substitutes, no compromises."

How do we find healing? We must take up the journey anew each day. What better day to recommit than today? No one else can do it for me. No one else can do it for you. Hillel expressed it succinctly, "If I don't do it, who will do it? If I don't do it right now, when will I do it?"

There are many photos about nature in this book – the animals, trees, shrubs, flowers, air and water that we can see from our home windows.

Wherever we are we see, hear, smell, taste and can feel the nature during the seasons of the year.

Kamarie's photos bring us closer to our own experiences of nature.

Enjoy them. Look for the details. Listen to the sounds of birds and the wind. Imagine what is happening. Taste the air after a rainstorm and smell the flowers and plants.

It's outside your own window. Imagine these things even when you cannot see them and thrive on the sensations your memories and imagination can create.

Nurture your relationships. We spend most of our life with people at work or at school or in our recreational activities who may not be there when we are most anxious and afraid.

The people we love, our pets and those who love us are often those we spend the least time with in our lives.

We need to reverse that trend.

We need to nurture our relationships as a top priority.

In the end, it is these relationships and the results from them that become our legacy and that help us feel whole; feel healed.

Healing Presence

My Seventh Friend

My first friend came and expressed her shock by saying, "I can't believe that you have cancer. I always thought you were so active and healthy." She left and I felt alienated and somehow very "different."

My second friend came and brought me information about a variety of cancer treatments. He said, "Whatever you do, don't take chemotherapy. It's a poison." He left and I felt scared and confused.

My third friend came and tried to answer my "whys" with the statement, "Perhaps God is disciplining you for some sin in your life." She left and I felt guilty.

My fourth friend came and told me, "If your faith is just great enough, God will heal you." He left and I felt that my faith must be inadequate.

My fifth friend came and told me to remember that "All things work together for good." She left and I felt angry.

My sixth friend never came at all. I felt sad and alone.

My seventh friend came and held my hand and said, "I care, I'm here. I want to help you through this." She left and I felt loved!

Linda MacRichardson, Robert Pope Foundation Newsletter, Fall 2002

Healing Breaths

Deep breathing, taking a brisk walk, doing relaxation exercises, tensing and relaxing our muscles are all ways to immediately relieve the pressure of stress. Deep breathing is one of the easiest techniques to master since it is useful at work, at home, while caught in traffic or on public transit, and at times when you cannot do any other techniques.

Deep breathing can take only 10 seconds or last a half-hour, depending on the circumstances. Regardless of the length, use it to the fullest and enjoy the feelings. Begin with short practices of a few minutes. You can always do longer sessions later on. Here's one method of deep breathing. There are different techniques and this one is one of the most popular.

1. Place your hands on your abdomen, right below the navel. The fingertips of each hand should touch one another.

2. Breathe in through your nose; it is healthier than breathing through your mouth because the air becomes humidified and doesn't irritate you, is filtered by the nostrils (breathing by mouth tends to lead to more bronchial and lung infections) and the air temperature is raised or lowered closer to your body temperature.

3. Inhale slowly; as you do, push the abdomen out as though it were a balloon expanding. With your eyes open or closed, "feel" the air passing through your nostrils.

4. As the abdomen expands, your diaphragm will move downward, allowing fresh air to enter the bottom of your lungs. Keep your back straight to aid the process of maximizing your breathing. Exhale through your nose or mouth, whichever is more comfortable.

5. As you continue to breathe imagine the air filling your lungs, your abdomen and, with each new breath, imagine the air filling your arms, legs and every part of your body. This will help you to concentrate on the various parts of your body and can help you to relax each area.

6. When you feel comfortable, take deeper breaths. Do not pause but allow the continuous flow of air through your body.

7. At first you should take as long to breathe in as you do breathing out. You might count in your head, "In -- one, two, three; Out -- one, two three." With practice, your breaths will be longer and deeper. Over time the ratio of breathing in and breathing out can become 1:2 to allow for the maximum expulsion of air and, therefore, the deeper and more cleansing the inhalation, "In -- one, two, three; Out -- one, two, three, four, five."

8. This counting in your head also helps you stay focused on the breathing rather than distracted. When you are distracted, don't worry about it. It's natural. Simply return to your counting. This takes practice but is well worth the effort.

9. Breaths should be silent unless you have nasal obstructions or other physical conditions that make your breathing louder.

10. Picture yourself in a place where you feel particularly comfortable (e.g., on a beach, on a nature walk, in a favorite room, playing a sport, in a childhood memory). Pick just one spot to concentrate on while you continue to breathe deeply for as long as you wish.

11. When you are ready, slowly begin to stretch your muscles as if you were yawning. As you feel more relaxed you can begin to return to "the real world" refreshed and whole.

Healing Attitudes

What we think usually affects what we do. If we believe the water glass is half-full, then we see life with a more positive attitude. If we see the glass as half-empty we are typically less satisfied with our lot in life. If we think to fill the glass before deciding, we know we can take control of our thoughts and that is the most empowering of all. Attitudes matter. Examine your own and see if any changes might give you a greater reason to get up in the morning and more gratitude at the end of your day.

Healing Places and Spaces

We all find comfort from places and spaces. It can be in our home, at a sporting event or movie, sitting quietly in nature, having a long hot shower, or the memory of a particular corner in a room in our childhood home. Wherever it is, you can bring it to mind no matter where you are. You are not restricted by places and spaces to feel healed. You can imagine it whenever and wherever you like.

Healing Movements

Moving feels good. Even if you are bedridden for a time, moving your arms and legs as much as you can and contracted-relaxing muscles feels good as you do them daily. If you are mobile you can walk, exercise, swim, play a sport, do tai chi or yoga. You can do it alone or with others. Movements, whatever is possible for you, give you a sense of control. Enjoy it often.

Jack Layton was a leading politician in Canada. We typically ignore much of what a politician has to say but Mr. Layton was dying and he wanted to leave a message to all Canadians – a message that most accepted as the gift it was meant to be. The letter was written only a few days before he died. His life in his last year was filled with healing – up to, and including, his last days at home surrounded by family and friends.

He ended his August 20, 2011 letter with: *My friends, love is better than anger. Hope is better than fear. Optimism is better than despair. So let us be loving, hopeful and optimistic. And we'll change the world.*

Healing: Kamarie's Thoughts

Healing. The process of healing. The meaning of healing. The idea of being healed. It means so many things to so many people. What does it mean to me? I'm not entirely sure. I am still on this journey. The definition changes on a daily basis. On my good days when mind and body and soul feel like they are all connected and communicating there is an indescribable sense of joy. You hit all the green lights and you find everything you need at the first store you go to and the dinner you make turns out better than you thought it would.

The bad days are when it takes every ounce of energy and will power just to throw back the covers and get out of bed. Feed the cat. Make coffee. Get dressed. Go to work. These are not healing days. These are days that you must just endure and get through knowing that tomorrow will be better.

I started having significant health problems about seven years ago when I turned 40. I seemed to be developing symptoms of diseases normally found in people 20-30 years older. Maybe I was just getting an early start. I've always been a bit of an overachiever. It soon became clear that I was going to be dealing with serious health problems that were going to require major changes in my daily life. After having the job of my dreams for 10 years I was no longer able to physically meet the demands it required of me and was forced to resign in order to continue to be able to walk. I healed from that through hours of physical therapy, treatments, rest and medication.

Then a year after that came the cancer diagnosis. Monday, February 13 2012. I had just come out of general anesthesia after having had major abdominal surgery to remove a grapefruit sized mass that was surrounding my left ovary. My surgeon came into my hospital room and stood as far away from me as he could while still being in the room as he coldly told me he was very sorry but it was cancer and the surgery had been much more extensive and invasive than they had first anticipated. I think he thought I was going to break down and cry and he needed to be poised for escape. I looked him straight in the eyes and said "OK, what do we do now?" He said I would need minimum six weeks recovery from the surgery and then we would hit it hard with chemotherapy to knock out whatever was left. I said "Alright, well, you know where to find me." I think he smiled. I'm not sure as I had never met him before that day.

Here I am now, almost four years later. After the first round of chemotherapy I went into complete and total remission for a year. The cancer had disappeared as if it had never been there in the first place. Then, a year later, almost to the day, it came back. I have been fighting it every single day since August of 2013. I have lost track of how many different cocktails of treatment we have tried. I will have a few infusions of the next drug on the list, then the side-effects take over and make continuing treatment impossible. We take a break to let my body recover. We try the next cocktail. The side-effects are worse than the drug. Over and over and over again. The tumors continue to grow. New ones appear. New medications are added to combat the side-effects that are horrible all on their own. I lose my hair three times over four years.

How does one even approach the idea of healing when every single day becomes its own challenge? I often think what I would do if my husband was enduring this and I was in his shoes, watching the person I love more than anything in the world suffer and endure constant pain and frustration. How would I cope? You start by keeping your life as "normal" as you can. You go to work when you feel well enough. You think about what to make for dinner on your way to the grocery store. You talk about your day over the table. You watch a movie together. You find humor in any situation you can. You take joy from the companionship of your pets that make your house a home filled with life. You cry. You yell. You scream and swear and never let anyone else see any of it. You go to bed and hope for peaceful, uninterrupted sleep so you can face the next day.

I deal with my cancer very honestly. I tell people who ask exactly what I am going through. If they don't want to know, then they shouldn't have asked in the first place. I do not play the "cancer card." I am not a victim. I am a person who unfortunately has been dealt a disease that no one should ever have to endure. It's no one's fault. There is no one to blame. You must choose to decide how you are going to face this and you must do what makes sense to you. No one can do it for you. I choose to keep moving forward, one step at a time. That does not mean that there are not days where I want to give up and just walk away from the treatments and the doctors and medications. I do. I have refused treatment on several occasions because I simply cannot face the thought of another round of sickening, poisoning chemo going through my body. I have anxiety attacks just driving to the clinic. The smell of the infusion center makes me want to be physically sick.

This past August when the cancer had progressed rapidly and aggressively my oncologist told me to think about the five things in my life that I value most. I knew exactly what she was saying. Start to think about what is important to you as you deal with the very real possibility of coming to the end of your life sooner than you thought. Even after everything I had endured over the last several years I had never thought that the cancer would be what would "get me" in the end. Now that is a very real possibility that must be faced. My husband and I have had brutally honest discussions about my death and my wishes. I will NOT make my family watch me die a long, painful death.

I will die with dignity, as much as that is in my control. How does thinking about death relate to healing, you may be asking yourself? Because, for me, by looking at this head on I can at least feel as though I have some measure of control over a small portion of my life and that allows me to move forward WITHOUT FEAR. This is healing for me. I will not live my life in pain and I will not give up my independence. This is healing for me. I will never take for granted a single moment when I feel good and can interact with my family and friends. This is healing for me. I want to dance when food tastes good and I actually look forward to a meal. This is healing for me. When I can make plans to see a friend and actually keep those plans. This is healing for me. When I have energy to work on my photos and do something creative. This is healing for me. When my husband and I talk about taking wonderful vacations to warm, tropical islands – even though we know we may never get there. This is healing for me. When my cat jumps up and curls up on my lap when I am crying and feeling sorry for myself. This is healing for me. When I have the opportunity to paint a canvas. This is healing for me. When I am in a frame of mind to actually be able to absorb and get lost in a good book. This is healing for me. When my real hair is long enough for me to do anything with it. This is healing for me. The list goes on and on. And that is the point. This list should go on. It should be endless.

Every cancer patient has a different story. Every person who deals with a deadly disease has a different story. My story may not resonate with you at all. That is all right. It doesn't have to. Your story is your own. Each of us must try to live our lives the best way we know how with the resources we have. I know how fortunate I am. I have a loving, supportive husband who has been my primary care giver for four years with no break. His job provides our only source of income. He is the strongest person I know. He smiles every day. He tells me he loves me every day. He goes to work every day to ensure that we can continue to live in our beautiful home and take vacations when the opportunity arises. He makes me laugh every day. He has never once made me feel like I was causing him stress. I could never have made it this far without him. We are in this together every step. And I have a truly amazing support group of family and friends that are there for me whenever I ask. They make all the difference on the days when I have had more than I think I can possibly stand.

Here is what I hope for you. I hope that by reading my story it has helped you clarify your own story. The things that are healing for me may not be healing for you. All I can tell you is that the most important aspect of personal healing is that if something brings you a sense of peace or allows you to feel like you are in control of even a small portion of your life, you should embrace it and never feel guilty about it. Having a disease like cancer gives you the right to be selfish, but only to a certain extent. Try not to let it define you. You are allowed to take time for yourself and allow yourself to rest and recover and recharge. It will take time. No one can tell you how much time. Only you can decide how and when you need to stop and take a "time out" for yourself. Be honest with yourself about what you need. Learn to listen to what your body is telling you. This has been the hardest part for me. I am still learning.

Healing is about learning to accept that although your life may be difficult and challenging you can always have some degree of control that allows you to decide how to move forward and get the most from what each day has to offer you. I wish you all the best in your search for what heals you.

Healing Spirit

Many people find healing through their spirituality. It is often most profound in moments of genuine silence, whether you are alone or with others. At a wedding as the bridal couple exchange rings. At the bedside as your loved one is sleeping. In a forest alone where the only sounds are distant birds and a rustling wind. These are moments of profound spirituality when we feel connected not only to those we love but to the earth, all its peoples, and the greater spirit that created it all.

Healing Thoughts

There are so many thoughts reflected through words that can inspire us; heal us. Thoughts through poetry and songs, through books and plays, and through the things people say to us. When you search for them, you will find them everywhere. When you think your own healing thoughts, you can identify those that are most helpful and pass them on to others so they, too, can benefit from your healing thoughts.

Healing Touch

There are few things as healing as a hug, a gentle touch of a hand and the grip of a strong person holding on to you for dear life. You can provide your own healing touch through a hot shower or long soak in the tub to let the water heal and surround you. You can allow others to hug you more often or go to a massage therapist for their healing touch. You can hold the hand of an elder or a child and feel their energy, strength and love flow through you.

Healing Care

Healing care is provided when both the person providing care and the person receiving it understand they are exchanging a mutual gift. Each benefits. If that is not true, then only providers of care are valued by society while the receivers are pitied. Whether you are the healing provider of care or the healing receiver – exchange your gifts freely, wholly, and lovingly.

Healing Prayers-Meditations

Zen Buddhist: *May I be free from fear. May I be happy. May I be filled with loving kindness.*

Jewish: *The higher wisdom is kindness.* [The Gemara, c 500 The Talmud, 276]

Christian: *Peace you give me. Your peace you give unto me. Not as the world giveth, giveth you unto me. I will not let my heart be weary, neither will I be afraid.*
(John 14:26)

Muslim: 900 years ago the mathematician-poet Omar Khayyam, in his confession of faith prayed: *Both thou and I are born alike, though some may sink and some may soar, we all are earth and nothing more.*

Pray not for things. Pray not for victory, protection or rescue. Pray to remind yourself to nurture friendships. Pray for courage. Pray for strength. Pray for perspective. Pray for love. Do this and never be disappointed again.

Healing Perspectives

Helen Keller, a woman extraordinarily familiar with life's difficulties wrote: *Although the world is full of suffering it is also full of the overcoming of it.* Find stories and personal examples of people who have overcome their suffering. As Henry Miller wrote: *We create our fate every day we live*, so start by creating your fate for just the rest of today and into tomorrow – one day at a time.

Healing Smiles

Smile. Smile as you think of someone you love or have loved. Smile to ease the confusion, the physical pain and the emotional trauma of what you are experiencing. Smile because it helps heal your body, your mind, and your spirit.

Healing Destiny

I do not know what your destiny
will be but this I do know…
You will always find happiness if
you seek and find how to
serve.
Albert E. Schweitzer

Healing – The Universal Rule

Healing oneself is similar to healing our global societies. Rather than concentrate on our differences, we need to concentrate on our similarities. We are all members of the human family and all of us need to be nurtured and all of us thrive on nurturing others. All of us want a home, enough food, schooling for our children and meaningful work for ourselves. One example of how we are all basically the same is the 'golden' rule as presented by the ancient religious texts.

Baha'i
Lay not on any soul a load that you would not wish to be laid upon you, and desire not for anyone the things you would not desire for yourself.
Baha u llah, Gleanings

Buddhism
Treat not others in ways that you yourself would find hurtful.
Undana-varqa: 518

Christianity
In everything, do to others as you would have them do to you; for this is the law and the prophets.
Jesus in Matthew 7:12

Confucianism
One word which sums up the basis of all good conduct…loving-kindness. Do not to others what you do not want done to yourself.
Analects, XV, 23

Hinduism
This is the sum of duty: do not do to others what would cause pain if done to you.
The Mahabharata 5:1517

Islam
No one of you truly believes until you wish for others what you wish for yourself.
The Prophet Muhammad, Hadith

Jainism
One should treat all creatures in the world as one would like to be treated.
Mahavira, Sutrakritanga

Judaism
What is hateful to you, do not to your neighbour. This is the whole Torah; all the rest is commentary.
Zhillel, The Talmud, Shabbat 31a

Native Spirituality
We are as much alive as we keep the earth alive.
Chief Dan George

Sikhism
I am a stranger to no one; and no one is a stranger to me. Indeed, I am a friend to all.
Guru Granth Sahib, pg. 1299

Taoism
Regard your neighbour's gain as your own gain, and your neighbour's loss as your own loss.
T'ai-shang Kan Ying P'ien, 213-218

Unitarianism
We affirm and promote respect for the interdependent web of all existence of which we are a part.
Unitarian Principle

Zoroastrianism
Do not do unto others whatever is injurious to yourself.
Shayast-na-Shayast 13.29

There is so much music available to us in the 21st century from our local garage band to international music of every description. Listen and perform the music that soothes you, excites you, comforts you and inspires you.

Healing Listening

There are few powers greater than the power that comes from listening to someone with your whole heart, mind and soul. Your genuine listening can heal someone who feels their worries and concerns are unheard. Your genuine listening can heal you too as you share in the experiences of others who may have travelled a similar journey to yours. Listen for the lessons others have to offer even when they do not know they are teaching you.

Healing Courage

Courage is not the towering oak that sees storms come and go–it is the fragile blossom that opens in the snow. – Alice M. Swain

Healing Stories

Written in 1513 by a thoughtful man who could be a Jew, a Christian, a Muslim, a Buddhist, a Hindu, or an atheist. All thoughtful women, men and children are gifts and we must treasure their stories as lessons for our own journeys.

I salute you. I am your friend, and my love for you goes deep.
There is nothing I can give you which you have not.
But there is much, very much, that, while I cannot give it, you can take.
No heaven can come to us unless our hearts find rest in it today. Take heaven!
No peace lies in the future which is not hidden in this present little instant. Take peace!

The gloom of the world is but a shadow. Behind it, yet within our reach, is joy. There is radiance and glory in darkness, could we but see. And to see, we have only to look. I beseech you to look!

Life is so generous a giver. But we, judging its gifts by their covering, cast them away as ugly or heavy or hard. Remove the covering, and you will find beneath it a living splendor, woven of love by wisdom, with power. Welcome it, grasp it, and you touch the angel's hand that brings it to you.

Everything we call a trial, a sorrow or a duty, believe me, that angel's hand is there. The gift is there and the wonder of an overshadowing presence.

Your joys, too, be not content with them as joys. They, too, conceal diviner gifts. Life is so full of meaning and purpose, so full of beauty beneath its covering, that you will find earth but cloaks your heaven. Courage then to claim it; that is all!

But courage you have, and the knowledge that we are pilgrims together, wending through unknown country home.

And so, at this time, I greet you, not quite as the world sends greetings, but with profound esteem and with the prayer that for you, now and forever, the day breaks and shadows flee away.

Healing Memories

Memories can give you flowers in wintertime and snowballs in summer. Memories of people you love can give you comfort when you feel alone and strength in a maddening crowd. Memories give you roots and wings to fly. Your memories can do whatever you want if you pay them attention and nurture new memories as often as you can.

Healing Reading and Writing

Reading books, magazine articles, plays, poetry, lyrics and Internet stories can all provides stories that help us see ourselves as whole; as healed. To make the stories real, write down a summary in a notebook to give you memories of success to help during dark days. Write down your own stories of success to inspire others.

Healing Stories

A young woman brings flowers to a nurse. She says, "You took care of my grandmother years ago. I was only 7 years old but you always had time for me. You always asked how I was doing. You always took the time to put your hand on my shoulder or even give me a hug when I was crying. You were there for me and I just wanted to thank you and give you a hug back. I'm not sure enough people think to hug you back."

What Next?

People are always looking for the trick or the next 'advanced' techniques to feeling whole; to feeling healed. It is age-old experiences, however, that are most likely to help you feel healed. It is the wisdom of those who have gone before you and learned how to heal that will provide you the best examples.

So before you read every book in the library, watch every DVD or television program on how to heal yourself – focus on the most basic elements described in this book. We do not have all the answers so we rely on those people through the centuries that have figured out some of these answers for us.

Concentrate on the basics. When you are ready, expand your knowledge and skills to an even deeper level of self-awareness and healing. Learn to understand, at the most profound level, your thoughts and how best to use them to become more whole, stronger, loving and, perhaps, healed.

It is in our rush to know everything that we procrastinate from doing even the most basic techniques that allow us to control our destiny.

Pick a few photos and a few thoughts from this book that touch you on a very personal level and concentrate your mind and heart on those, today. That really is the key to "what next."

We may never be 'completely healed' – whatever that means. But we can be more healed than we feel now. We can be more healed than we imagined. Whether we get cured, or not, of our illness or condition is less important than becoming healed. When one is healed, even when we are dying, we become whole and create a wonderful gift to everyone around us.

Kamarie Livingston was born in Colorado but moved to Canada when she was a teenager and did all of her secondary and university education in Ontario, where her heart lies always. She is a "dabbling" photographer, a hobby inspired by her late step-father, Lynn Davie. She lives in Minneapolis, Minnesota with her husband of 21 years, Michael, their African Grey parrot, Oliver, and cat, Harley. Kamarie works part-time when she can, travels and loves to watch the birds and other animals outside her window. For the past year (2015), while undergoing treatment for cancer, Kamarie has taken a photo a day as her commitment to do something creative every day. This book's photos come from that effort. She is a four-year cancer survivor who is determined to make the most of what life has to offer.

Harry van Bommel is the author of over 50 books in the fields of family caregiving, hospice palliative care, healthcare navigation, and family history. He helped both of his parents and grandfather live at home until they died. His caregiving books are available for free online reading at **www.carelibrary.com** and can be purchased through **www.legacies-inc.com**. His Canada 150 Project: *Our Canada, Our Stories – Notre Canada, Nos Histoires* is at **www.canada150.ca**.

Made in the USA
Las Vegas, NV
08 November 2026

57690466R00031